# About the Mass

## Les Miller

NOVALIS

© 2010 Novalis Publishing Inc.

Cover design: Mardigrafe
Cover illustration: Audrey Wells
Interior photographs: © WP Wittman Photography
Layout: Mardigrafe and Audrey Wells
Reviewed by Msgr. Dennis Murphy, founder of the Institute
for Catholic Education

Published by Novalis

Publishing Office
10 Lower Spadina Avenue, Suite 400
Toronto, Ontario, Canada
M5V 2Z2

Head Office
4475 Frontenac Street
Montréal, Québec, Canada
H2H 2S2

www.novalis.ca

Library and Archives Canada Cataloguing in Publication

Miller, Leslie, 1952-
     25 questions about the Mass / Les Miller.

ISBN 978-2-89646-219-3

     1. Mass. I. Title. II. Title: Twenty-five questions about the Mass.

BX2230.3.M54          2010 264'.02036          C2010-902198-3

Printed in Canada.

We acknowledge the financial support of the Government of Canada through
the Book Publishing Industry Development Program (BPIDP) for our publishing
activities.

5   4   3   2   1      14   13   12   11   10

# TABLE OF CONTENTS

# A Word from the Author

At every moment of every day, a Mass is taking place somewhere in the world. Millions of people are reaching out to God with prayers, songs and actions. Catholics have been celebrating the Mass for 2,000 years. Why? As Roman Catholics, we believe that God is powerfully present in the Mass. The Mass is our central act of worship. Here we can connect with God in a very deep way.

This book invites you to learn more about the Mass. If you understand the Mass better, this can help make your faith stronger. We will explore this subject through 25 questions that young people often ask about the Mass. Read through the questions in order, or start with the ones that you find yourself asking. Talk about them with your family and your friends. (Check out the back of this book, too. It gives an overview of the Mass and a list of words to know.)

By the way, having questions about the Mass is a good thing! There's always more to find out about our faith.

May God bless your journey to the heart of the Catholic faith. See you at Mass sometime soon!

# Why *do we go to Mass?*

There are lots of answers to this question. All of them can give us part of the picture. Let's see if we can fit some of the pieces together.

The Mass is sometimes called "the great prayer of the Church." A prayer is an action that puts us in touch with God. We can talk to God, listen to God or simply feel God's presence with us. The Mass is a time where many prayers are woven together to create a beautiful tapestry of worship. In the Mass, we draw near to God in a number of ways:

- in the prayers and responses we say aloud together
- in the songs we sing
- in the readings we listen to from God's word, the Bible
- in the presence of Jesus in the Eucharist
- in the prayers to the Holy Spirit to make holy the bread, the wine and the people of God
- in seeing the goodness of God in each other.

Some people say that Mass gives them a sense of peace and beauty. Mass is a place where heaven feels very near to us. Sometimes at Mass we feel close to people we love who have died. Once a week we can go to a place where we know for sure that we belong to God and we belong to each other. We find God in our hearts, but we also find God in each other and most powerfully in the sacrament of the Eucharist.

Some people remind us that it is our duty as Catholics to go to Mass. It is a duty, but in a good way. At the Last Supper, Jesus asked us to remember him by eating the bread of life. The Church expects us to do this at least once a week and on special days such as Christmas and New Year's Day. Catholics have been remembering Jesus in this way for 2,000 years. As one person said, "Who am I to stop 2,000 years of history and tradition?"

 The Mass is also called the Eucharist. We say *Eucharist* when we talk about the sacrament. The word *Eucharist* comes from the Greek word *eucharistia*, which means "thanksgiving." At Mass, we give thanks to God for our many blessings.

 For Roman Catholics, a sacrament is one of the seven rituals that brings us into God's presence in a deep and special way. The seven sacraments are Baptism, Confirmation, Eucharist, Reconciliation, Holy Orders, Marriage, and Anointing of the Sick.

The word *Mass* probably comes from the words said at the end of the Mass. In Latin, this phrase is *Ite, missa est*. The words literally mean "*Go, it is the dismissal.*" In other words, "Continue God's mission for you in your daily life."

??????????? **2** ???????????

## Why *do we celebrate* Mass in church on Sunday?

Jewish people observe the Sabbath, the day of rest and worship, from sunset on Friday to sunset on Saturday. Roman Catholics observe the Lord's Day on Sunday. How this happened takes us to the heart of understanding the Mass.

In the story of creation, God worked for six days and rested on the seventh. In the Ten Commandments, the third one asks us to rest on the seventh day of the week and keep it holy. The resurrection of Jesus took place on Easter Sunday, the first day of the week. Early Christians gathered on the first day of the week to remember Jesus in the early celebrations of the Eucharist. Since Easter is the most important feast for Christians, the Church decided that Sunday would be our day of rest and worship.

Sunday is a day when we can connect with God, our family and our parish community. It's a time to say thanks to God, to open up our hearts and remember that we are God's children.

For religious Jews of long ago, a day started at sunset and ended at sunset on the next day. That is why the Jewish Sabbath starts on Friday evening and ends on Saturday evening. The Roman Empire ruled the world of the early Christians. Romans understood a day as being from midnight to the next midnight.

Some people think that Christians changed the Sabbath to Sunday because they were adapting to Roman customs. This isn't true. Romans didn't even have a seven-day week until 300 years after Jesus lived! When Christianity became more popular in the Roman Empire, the Romans decided that Sunday would be a day of rest and worship.

????????? **3** ?????????????

## How do we prepare for Mass?

There's a difference between a routine and a ritual. A routine is something we do regularly but don't always have to think too much about. For example, we brush our teeth every morning and every night without thinking about it. That's a routine. Mass is different. It is a ritual. Rituals have deep meaning attached to them. Because we meet God in a special way at Mass, we need to prepare ourselves in a special way.

The Church asks us to prepare our bodies and souls for Mass. Some people like to wear nicer clothes to Mass because they feel this is a special time. There are no Church rules about what to wear, but dressing up a bit is one way to get ready. Some people like to read the readings for that Sunday and think about God's word before they go to Mass. Also, we are not to eat anything for an hour before receiving the Eucharist, unless we need to eat for a medical reason.

When we enter the church, we dip our fingers in a basin of holy water and bless ourselves in the name of the Father, and of the Son, and of the Holy Spirit. This gesture reminds us of our Baptism, when we were baptized with water that had been blessed by the priest.

Then we go to our seats, which are usually benches set up in rows. The benches are called pews. Before we sit, we face the tabernacle, where Jesus, in the form of the Blessed Sacrament, is present. At this time we bend and kneel on one knee for a few seconds. This is called "genuflecting" and is a sign of reverence for God.

Once we take our places in the pew, we prepare for Mass by praying. Many people kneel at this time. We can pray formal prayers such as the Our Father, the Hail Mary or the Glory Be, or we can ask God in our own words to help prepare our hearts for Mass.

Holy water is blessed each year at the Easter Vigil. The bottom of the large candle that is a sign of the light of Christ is dipped in the water. This water is used through the Church year in baptisms and other rituals.

When you go into the church, it is best not to talk. Being quiet shows respect for God and for other people. Silence allows us to focus on our relationship with God without distractions. Silence reminds us that this is a sacred place.

The tabernacle is found near the front of the church, off to one side. It looks like a box with a door in it. It is usually quite fancy. Inside the tabernacle are consecrated hosts – the hosts that the Holy Spirit made holy at an earlier Mass. The tabernacle can be traced back to the time of Moses, many thousands of years ago. The Ten Commandments were kept in the tabernacle (or ark) in those days. It was the most sacred object for the Jewish people. For us today, Jesus, who is present in the Eucharist, is the most holy sign of God's love.

# Why do we stand, sit and kneel at times in the Mass?

You go to Mass. You kneel. You sit. You stand. You sit. You kneel. Sometimes it feels like a workout! Why do we keep changing positions?

Prayer is all about communicating with God. We often use words or thoughts to pray, but we can also pray through our actions. This is sometimes called body prayer. Through our gestures and body position, we communicate with God in prayer.

We make the sign of the cross several times during the Mass to connect ourselves with the death of Jesus on the cross and to identify ourselves as Christians.

When the Romans saw the early Christians kneeling in prayer, they were shocked. They thought it was shameful to be in the position of slaves or defeated enemies. But Christians took the practice of kneeling from the Scriptures. It was a common prayer position for the Jewish people. Kneeling was a way of showing that we are humble before God and that we are servants of God's love. Kneeling is a sign of deep respect for God.

Another way to show respect is to stand. For example, we stand to sing O Canada. At Mass, we stand to listen to the Gospel, where we meet Jesus in the reading. We also stand for other key moments of the Mass.

 We bow our heads in prayer as a sign of respect.

 During the sharing of the sign of peace at Mass, we greet, shake hands with or hug people to wish them peace. This practice goes back to the earliest days of the Church.

## Why do priests sometimes use symbols such as water, oil and incense?

Many symbols that have deep meaning are used during the Mass. A symbol is something that tells a story. For example, during the opening procession at Mass, someone may carry a large cross. This reminds us that Jesus died on the cross. Also, the book of scripture readings (the *Lectionary*) may be held high during the procession. This book reminds us that God is present in the readings. Other symbols are water, oil and incense.

At certain times of the year, the priest may sprinkle us with *water* during Mass to remind us of our Baptism. You probably don't remember your Baptism, but you had holy water poured over you on that day. Water is a powerful symbol that is used in many faiths around the world. We use water each day to wash our bodies. In Baptism, we use water as a sign of sharing the life of Jesus and to purify our souls. Water brings life to living things. God gives us eternal life.

Thousands of years ago, the Israelites poured *oil* on a prophet's or king's head to show that the person was holy. In the Gospels, you can read the story of the woman who poured oil on the head of Jesus. In fact, the word "Christ" comes from the Greek word for "anointed" or "being given holy oil." In Baptism and Confirmation, we are anointed with sacred oil on our foreheads. This oil is a sign of our holiness.

*Incense* is another symbol that goes back to biblical times. During those times, the people used sweet-smelling smoke to purify the space where they worshipped. They believed that heaven was a physical place up in the sky, and that the incense would rise to heaven. Today, we believe that incense is a way of showing honour and reverence to God.

 Moses built a golden altar for burning incense near the entrance to the tent where the Ark of the Covenant was kept. The Ark was a kind of tabernacle. Inside the Ark were the Ten Commandments. (To learn more about Moses, see *25 Questions about the Founders of the World's Major Religions*.)

 Bells are sometimes rung during the Mass when the bread and wine are being transformed into the body and blood of Jesus. This practice goes back to Jewish customs and to a Christian tradition in the Middle Ages. Some people couldn't attend Mass because they were sick or had other duties. The bells were rung both inside and outside the church to announce that something special was happening.

 At Mass, candles are a symbol of the light of Christ. Christ brings light into the dark places of our lives.

# Why *does the priest wear robes?*

At Mass, we know right away who the priest is because of the long robes he wears. If you look closely, you will see several things that are symbols of his role.

The priest usually gets ready for Mass in a side room off the altar called the *sacristy*. Often, he first puts on the *alb*, which is a light white garment. The alb comes from the linen tunics that the Romans wore. It is white to remind us of the new life and purity of Baptism. Sometimes other people who help with the liturgy, such as the deacon, the ministers of communion, the altar servers, and the choir will wear an alb. A shorter form of the alb is called a *surplice*.

On top of the alb, the priest wears a *chasuble*. This heavier layer is like a cloak with no sleeves. It was first worn as an outer garment during Roman times, to protect people from the weather when they were riding a horse or walking. Today, chasubles come in different colours. Each colour has its own meaning:

- Green is used for much of the year, at times when there is no special day or season.
- Violet or purple is a sign of something solemn or serious, and is used in Advent and Lent.

- White is the colour of purity and joy. It is used during the Christmas and Easter seasons, at Masses where there are baptisms, weddings or funerals, and on some feast days.

- Red is the colour of the Holy Spirit and of martyrdom. It is used on Pentecost, Good Friday, and feast days of saints who died for their faith in God.

The long, narrow strip of cloth around the priest's neck is called a *stole*. It is a sign that the priest has a special role of teaching, guiding and blessing in the Church. (Deacons wear a stole over their alb to show they have a special role, too.) There are two stories about the stole. One story traces it back to the prayer shawl (tallit) that Jewish men wear during worship. The other story links the stole to the cloth that Jesus used to wash the feet of the disciples at the Last Supper.

Some priests wear a long robe called a *cassock* both at Mass and in their other official duties. It is often black. Bishops have purple cassocks and the Pope wears a white cassock.

Often when a priest visits a school, he will wear a black shirt with a black collar that has a strip of white showing at the front. This is called a roman collar. It is made to look like a cassock that has a collar attached to it.

In some parishes, a deacon may assist the priest at Mass. The deacon has special training to serve the members of the Church. He can also give the homily, baptize people and preside at funerals and weddings.

## What are the main parts of the Mass?

The Mass has two main parts: the *Liturgy of the Word* and the *Liturgy of the Eucharist*. *Liturgy* is an ancient word that means "public work." For the first Christians, liturgy was the public worship of the Church. Public worship included different tasks, such as serving the poor and spreading the Gospel.

Here is the order of what happens in the Mass:

+ the Introductory Rites
+ the Liturgy of the Word
+ the Liturgy of the Eucharist
+ the Concluding Rite.

During the Introductory Rites, the priest and the people who assist him enter the church in a procession while everyone sings the entrance hymn. In this part of the Mass, we admit that we need God's love and forgiveness. On Sundays (except in Advent and Lent) we sing a song of praise to God called the *Gloria*. Then the priest prays the opening prayer.

During the *Liturgy of the Word,* we meet God in scripture. In this part of the Mass, we do a number of things:

- we listen to the readings from scripture
- we listen to the priest's homily, where he speaks about the readings and what they mean for us in our daily lives
- we stand and say the Creed, which sums up our beliefs
- we bring forward our needs as the people of God in the Prayer of the Faithful.

*The Liturgy of the Eucharist* comes next. Here is what happens at this time:

- The altar is prepared and the bread and wine are carried up.
- The Mass is a memorial meal that recalls the Last Supper and makes present Jesus, who gave his life for us. The Eucharistic Prayer refers to this event and calls on the Holy Spirit to change the bread and wine into the Body and Blood of Christ. At the end of the Eucharistic Prayer, we sing or say "Amen."
- During the Communion Rite, we pray the Our Father aloud together, share a sign of peace, and pray the Lamb of God prayer. Then we receive communion, sharing in the presence of Jesus in the most special way.

After communion, in the Concluding Rite, the priest blesses us and sends us out to serve God in our daily lives.

You can read more about each part of the Mass in this book.

Mass is usually celebrated at the parish church, which is the centre of our faith community. Sometimes Mass is celebrated in other places, such as a school, an arena or even a field when everyone can't fit inside the church.

The Mass is sometimes called a *sacrifice*. In ancient times, Jewish people sacrificed an animal on an altar to honour God. Christianity changed this practice. Jesus saw himself as a sacrificial lamb, so there was no more need to sacrifice animals in this way.

The Introductory Rites begin the Mass. The Concluding Rite ends the Mass. *Rite* is another word for *ritual*.

# Why do we sing at Mass?

We usually start the Mass by standing and singing a hymn together. The Bible tells us to "make a joyful noise to God," so we sing at Mass to praise God and to thank God. Although the choir may lead the singing, everybody joins in, even if their voices are less than perfect. Hymns were written to be sung in God's worship. Other parts of the Mass that are often sung are the Gloria, the Holy, Holy, the Great Amen and the Lamb of God.

St. Augustine, one of the great teachers of the Church who lived over 1500 years ago, said that to sing is to pray twice. It's true. When we sing, we speak to God in words. But we also communicate with God through music, which can sometimes say more than words. When we sing, the beauty we experience links us with the choirs of heaven. Singing also gives us a sense of unity with each other. We are in harmony with each other.

 One of the oldest forms of Church music is Gregorian chant, which was written over 1400 years ago! Monks used to sing chant during their times of prayer. (It is called Gregorian after Pope Gregory I, who asked that Church music be simplified so it was easier to learn.) Gregorian chant is still popular among Christians and non-Christians because it is sacred and peaceful. You can find examples of this kind of singing on YouTube.

 Many older hymns were written in Latin. Until 1965, much of the Mass was in Latin. (Latin was the language of the Romans.) Although for many centuries it was helpful for everyone throughout the world to use the same language for the Mass, that changed in recent times. Most people today don't understand Latin. Church leaders decided that it was more important for people to understand the words than to feel connected to the past or to have a common Church language.

## Why do we start the Mass by telling God we are sorry?

If we go on vacation, we pack our suitcases ahead of time. If we are going to play an important game, we practise and train. For important events in our lives, we prepare. Meeting God in the Mass also means preparing. So we start the Mass by singing together, blessing ourselves with the sign of the cross, and then checking in with ourselves to look at our state of mind. This check-in is called the Penitential Rite.

We know that we are not always loving, fair and understanding. We may have hurt others or ourselves. This is the time to be honest with ourselves and with God. We admit that our actions have hurt our relationships with others, with God and with ourselves. This is what we call "sin." God knows our sins – we can't hide them from God. We don't say these sins out loud, but we are aware of them.

If the sin is deep and the relationship with God, others and ourselves is broken, we need the sacrament of Reconciliation. During the sacrament, we tell the priest how we have sinned and he absolves or releases us from our sin. Then we can start over with a clean slate, and "sin no more." It is a good habit to go to Reconciliation regularly, to ask God to forgive us for our sins and to help us do better from that moment on.

A prayer we often say during the Penitential Rite is the *Confiteor*:

I confess to almighty God, and to you, my brothers and sisters, that I have sinned through my own fault,
in my thoughts and in my words,
in what I have done, and in what I have failed to do;
and I ask blessed Mary, ever virgin,
all the angels and saints, and you, my brothers and sisters,
to pray for me to the Lord our God.

Sometimes during this part of the Mass the priest will sprinkle the congregation with holy water to remind us of our baptismal promises, instead of saying the Confiteor together.

To conclude the Penitential Rite, we say, "Lord, have mercy. Christ, have mercy. Lord, have mercy." This prayer is known as the *Kyrie*. Many of the earliest Christians spoke Greek, and this prayer began in Greek. In fact, the original Greek is often used at Mass: *Kýrie eléison; Christé eléison; Kýrie eléison.*

# Why *do we listen to readings that were written so long ago?*

The Bible was indeed written long ago. It has two main parts. The first part – the *Hebrew Scriptures* or *Old Testament* – tells the story of God and the Jewish people. The second part – the *Christian Scriptures* or *New Testament* – tells the story of Jesus and the early Church. The message of the Bible may be old, but it is very important: it tells us how people met God then and how we can meet God in our lives today.

The *First Reading* is usually from the Old Testament or Hebrew Scriptures (except during the Easter season, when it is from the Acts of the Apostles, in the New Testament). We listen to a part of the story of the Jewish people as they grew in their understanding of their relationship with God.

The *Responsorial Psalm* is sung or read. (It is called "responsorial" because it is a response to the First Reading.) There are 150 Psalms in the Old Testament. These prayer "songs" were written up to 3,000 years ago. We hear in them words of joy and sorrow, thanksgiving and praise, pleading and comfort.

The *Second Reading* usually comes from the letters of St. Paul or another New Testament writer. It often gives us advice about how we as Christians should live and worship together.

Then the priest proclaims the *Gospel,* the "Good News" of Jesus Christ, from the New Testament. There are four Gospels: the Gospel according to Matthew, Mark, Luke or John. We know that this is the most important reading for these reasons:

- People stand up for the Gospel to show respect.
- We begin with a short song of praise called the *Gospel Acclamation*.

- We bless ourselves with the *little Sign of the Cross*, tracing a small cross on our forehead, our lips and our heart while silently saying, "May Christ's words be in my mind, on my lips, and in my heart."
- The Gospel is read by the priest or the deacon.

The priest then connects the readings to our everyday life in a short talk called the *homily*. Although the words from the readings were written long ago, they form a sure path to living in faith, hope and love.

 The book of scripture readings is called the *Lectionary*.

 The Church has a three-year cycle of Sunday readings. In Year A, most of the readings we listen to come from the Gospel according to Matthew. In Year B, most are from the Gospel according to Mark. In Year C, most are from the Gospel according to Luke. We listen to the Gospel according to John at certain times each year, especially around Lent and Easter.

## What is the Creed?

After the *homily,* the people gathered at Mass stand up as a sign of unity and respect. They say the *Apostles' Creed* or the *Nicene Creed* aloud together. These are statements about our faith that we all agree on. They are the basics of our beliefs. Each creed has three parts. The first part states our belief in God the Father, the Creator. The second part states our belief in Jesus Christ, God's Son and our Saviour. The third part states our belief in the Holy Spirit, who guides the Church and each of our lives.

These statements were written during the time of the early Church. The Church has kept them ever since.

People used to think the Apostles' Creed was written by the apostles, who were followers of Jesus. While this may not be historically true, these statements are an inspired summary of the apostles' teachings. The Apostles' Creed has twelve parts: one for each of the apostles.

The Nicene Creed came from the Council of Nicea in the year 325. Some people questioned whether Jesus was divine. This challenge allowed the Church to state clearly that Jesus is fully God even though he is fully human. Also, we believe in one God in three persons: the Father, the Son and the Holy Spirit.

In the Mass, you will hear God called "Father." This language comes to us from the Bible and the Church. The Church teaches that God cannot be easily summed up in human words. "Father" does not capture who God is. No one word can. The Church doesn't use the name "Father" to say that males are better than females. It is a way of understanding that God is like a loving yet powerful parent. (You might wonder why we don't call God "Mother." Actually, the image of God as a mother does appear from time to time in the Bible!) In recent years, people have looked for different images for God, beyond Father and Mother, that reflect our modern ways of thinking.

## Why do we pray together for people we don't even know?

We stay standing while the reader or deacon leads us in prayer for our human needs. This is called the *Prayer of the Faithful*. Each part of it is called a *petition*. These petitions follow a pattern. We pray for

- the needs of the Church
- leaders and nations
- people who are suffering in some way
- our local Church community (this may include prayers for the sick and for people who have died).

We pray to God not to change God's mind or focus God's attention on these people. God already knows what the needs are. We pray to bring the people into our relationship with God, so that with God's help we can help them.

We can pray for anyone or anything in need of God's care, including ourselves.

Sometimes at Mass, the priest will invite the people to say their personal prayers of petition out loud.

People who read the Scriptures and the Prayer of the Faithful at Mass stand at a podium called an *ambo*.

# LITURGY OF THE EUCHARIST

**13**

## Why do we collect money at Mass? Where does the money go?

At Mass each Sunday, money is collected to help support the Church and people in need. The Catholic Church helps the poor around the world in spiritual and financial ways. The money you put into the collection basket not only pays for lights and heat for the church, but also is used to buy food for the hungry and to care for people who are suffering. The collection of money during Mass reminds us that our time of worship is connected to our work as Christians to help bring the message of Jesus to the world.

- The people who collect the money are called *Ministers of Hospitality* or *Ushers*.

- The Roman Catholic Church is the largest organization in the world that helps the poor. It gives money directly but also through organizations such as hospitals and schools.

- In the early days of the Church, people would bring food and drink to give to the needy in their community.

# What is carried up during the Offertory Procession?

As we prepare for the Eucharist, the priest gets the altar ready. Two people walk up the centre aisle of the church carrying the bread and wine that will become the body and blood of Christ during the Mass. This is called the Offertory Procession.

The bread that is carried in the procession is not the type of bread we get from a bakery. This bread is made without yeast, so it doesn't rise. (It reminds us of the Passover meal that Jesus celebrated at the Last Supper. During the Passover, the Israelites didn't have time to let their bread rise because they had to escape from Egypt.)

The wine that is carried in the procession also reminds us of the Passover meal. At the Last Supper, Jesus said that when we drink the wine in his memory, we become one with him.

Bread is made from wheat flour. Wheat is one of the most common grains and is the key ingredient of "our daily bread." It is something that is for everyone, just like the Gospel.

The bread (also called hosts) is put in a vessel called a *ciborium*. The wine is poured into a *chalice*. A drop of water is added to the wine.

The priest and the congregation say several prayers to prepare for the Eucharistic Prayer. Just as we say grace before meals, at Mass we give thanks for the spiritual food that we will receive.

A special book called a *Sacramentary* is placed on the altar at this time. This book contains the words for the prayers that the priest says during the Eucharistic Prayer.

# What happens in the Eucharistic Prayer?

The *Eucharistic Prayer* is a collection of a few shorter prayers. The priest connects the season of the Church year with the Eucharist in a prayer called the *Preface*.

Together we say the *Holy, Holy*, a song of praise from the Old Testament. Then we kneel as a sign of respect. The priest chooses from a few different Eucharistic Prayers. Each one recalls the Last Supper and Jesus' words to remember him in the Eucharist.

This is a long prayer because there is so much to say about the people who gather with God. We remember the saints and all good people who are in God's loving embrace. In a special way, we remember people who have died.

Everyone in the church takes part in the Eucharistic Prayer by saying the responses. At one point, the priest lifts up the host and later the chalice. The prayer asks that the Holy Spirit change the bread and wine into the body and blood of Jesus.

At the end of the Eucharistic Prayer, the priest gives thanks and praise to God. He says or sings these words with joy. We answer, "Amen!" That means "I agree!"

Some people think a prayer service is the same as a Mass. They do have many things in common: people gathered for prayer and worship, scripture, song, rituals and the desire to get closer to God. What makes a Mass different is the consecration of the Eucharist. At a prayer service, any leader of a community can lead it. At a Mass, only the priest can.

The action of changing the bread and wine into the body and blood of Jesus is called *consecration*, meaning "to make holy."

## (16)

# Why do we say the Our Father or Lord's Prayer together?

One of the first prayers we learn is the Our Father, also called the Lord's Prayer. We pray this prayer at Mass for a few reasons:

- It is the prayer that Jesus taught his disciples to pray. It brings all Christians together in Christ.
- Christians have been praying it since Jesus taught it long ago. It brings Christians together through time.
- People of many languages and cultures pray this prayer. At every second of the day, someone in the world is praying the Our Father.

The word "hallowed" is in the Our Father: "hallowed be your name." This old English word means "holy" or "saintly." It is part of the word *Halloween*, which is short for *All Hallows Eve* (because it is the evening before All Saints' Day, November 1).

? ? ? ? ? ? ? ? ? ? **17** ? ? ? ? ? ? ? ? ?

# Why *do* we shake hands with *people* during Mass?

The early Christians held their celebrations of the Eucharist in people's homes, often in secret. (In those days, it was against the law to be a Christian.) When they began to worship, they gave each other a holy kiss of peace. Over time, this ritual faded away. In the 1960s, the Church brought back the sign of peace.

After we pray the Our Father, the priest wishes us peace and he or the deacon invites us to share a sign of peace with each other. The people shake hands or hug each other. This is another sign of unity. We have just spoken words of unity during the Our Father, and now we put our words into action. We don't just pray for peace, we take real steps to be at peace with each other. We need to show signs of peace outside the Mass in our daily lives as well.

For Christians, peace is important. If we want peace in the world, we have to start living in a peaceful way with our family, our friends and our classmates. We can also pray for peace.

????????? **18** ????????????

# What happens during communion?

The priest lifts up the host and tells us that it is the Lamb of God who takes away the sins of the world. Remember that the Mass is also a sacrifice. Jesus gave up his life so that all of us can have eternal life.

We line up to receive the Eucharist. Usually, we receive just the body of Christ, but sometimes we can also receive the blood of Christ. The priest or one of the ministers of communion holds the body of Christ in front of you and says, "The body of Christ." You say, "Amen." Usually the host is placed in your left hand. With your right hand you place it reverently on your tongue right away. You return to your pew and pray silently for a few minutes.

The word "communion" means our sharing together in Eucharist. Communion is an act of sharing.

Some people do not receive the host. Instead, they cross their hands on their chest to ask for a blessing. They may be too young to receive communion, not Catholic, or in need of the sacrament of Reconciliation to prepare to receive the Eucharist.

After communion, the priest wipes out the sacred vessels (the *ciborium* and the *chalice*) with a cloth. The altar server puts them on a side table. If any consecrated hosts are left, they are placed in the tabernacle, the beautifully decorated container near the altar. They are used at another time.

# Why does the priest bless us at the end of Mass?

At the end of Mass, in the Concluding Rite, we are given a mission: to share God's love, which we have experienced in the Mass, with the world. The priest sends us on this important mission when he blesses us.

We can also bless ourselves and the people in our lives. Blessings remind us that God is with us. When we make the sign of the cross, we are asking God to bless us. We ask for God's blessing at meals. Many parents bless their young children at bedtime. The response to a blessing is "Amen."

 Sometimes at Mass, there is a solemn blessing where we bow our heads and say "Amen" three times.

 A famous blessing comes from the Old Testament. It is said by Aaron, the brother of Moses:

> May the Lord bless you and take care of you;
> May the Lord be kind and gracious to you;
> May the Lord look on you with favour and give you peace.
> (Numbers 6:24-26)

?????????? **20** ??????????

# What if I find Mass boring?
# What can I do?

Have you ever tried to watch a TV show in a language you don't understand? It just doesn't grab you – you don't know what's going on. It's the same for the Mass. To get something out of it, you need to know what different things mean. The Mass is loaded with symbolism. If you don't get what the symbols mean, it isn't going to be as rich an experience as it could be. The trick is to figure out the meaning of the symbols by reading books like this one!

Even the words we use at Mass can be a challenge, because some are words we don't use every day: words like Eucharist, homily, hallowed, and offertory. Knowing what the words mean can help you understand what is going on. (At the end of this book is a list of words to know. Check it out!)

Once you understand the symbols better, you can enter into the Mass in a deeper way. Now the Mass won't be so much about what the words mean or what the symbols stand for, but about what happens inside you when you're there. Some people feel peaceful at Mass: they know that this is where they belong. They feel about as close to God as a person on earth can feel. Mass is a safe place where they don't have to worry about any troubles or sadness they might have. Other feelings people have at Mass are joy, love, connection to a community, and hope. That's amazing!

At Mass, we aren't just sitting and watching things happen, as if we are at a movie. There is no audience at Mass. We are all part of the action. The priest leads it, but we all have important roles to play. With the priest, we offer our praise and worship to God. We sing, move in a procession to the altar for communion, and pray together. Young people who want to get even more involved can be altar servers, take part in children's liturgy, or join a choir.

## What does Mass have to do with my daily life?

Sometimes Mass doesn't seem to have anything to do with your "real" life. What do singing hymns, kneeling and being blessed have to do with what happens when you hang out with friends, play sports, spend time with your family or go to school?

The answer is "Lots!" Many wise people have thought about this question. They say that the Mass gives us these things:

- *Wisdom for daily life*. The Scriptures and the homily connect us with deep wisdom about how to live with dignity, wisdom and kindness. The value of human life is raised up in a world that often tries to tear it apart.

- *Spiritual fuel for our journey*. We need food, clothing, shelter and companionship to live. But we also need meaning and purpose. Going to Mass regularly reminds us of our real purpose in life: loving God, our neighbour and ourselves.

- *Companionship*. Mass is a time to gather with others. We know that we are not alone on our journey. Other people can help us.

- *A sense of who we are*. Jesus is the centre of our life. To stay true to ourselves, we need to stay connected to Jesus.

- *A place to celebrate and a place to mourn*. In silent prayer and out loud, we thank God at Mass for our gifts and blessings. Getting into the habit of giving thanks helps us not to become selfish or spoiled. The Mass also gives us a place to mourn – to admit that we are hurt, angry or upset. In prayer, we get closer to God, who knows our sorrows.

The Mass connects to our life in many ways. The homily links scripture and everyday life. We pray for the world and for people in need during the Prayer of the Faithful. We collect money for the Church to help others. We are blessed at the end of the Mass so we can be Christ's hands and feet for the world today.

## What can I say to my friends who make fun of me for going to Mass?

Going to church isn't as popular as it used to be. Sometimes you have to have courage to say that you go to Mass if your friends don't. But it has always been that way for Christians. It's all about you and your relationship with God. Your faith helps make you who you are. It has helped form you and shape you. If your friends like you for who you are, the Church has helped you to be that way. Take away the Church and you become a different person.

Some people don't go to Mass because they don't want to be seen doing something that their friends don't do. Humans need to belong to groups and do what the group does. If going to Mass isn't one of those defining things, they will find it hard to understand.

Just remember that friendships are important, but your relationships with God and your family are even more important. Tell your friends, "That's just part of who I am – a Catholic." If they are true friends, they'll respect your choices.

Some people say that religion and faith are unscientific. After all, no one can prove that God exists! But some of the most important scientific discoveries have been made by religious people. For example, Fr. Gregor Mendel's work on plants led to the study of genetics. Catholics believe that faith and science can work together to help all people.

Some people believe that religion causes wars. But the core teachings of all the world religions promote peace. If any group uses aggressive military force in the name of religion, then its members are not being true to the teachings of their faith.

# ??????????? 23 ???????????

## I'm a good person...
## Do I still need to go to Mass?

A popular saying from a few years ago was "God doesn't make junk!" God loves and values every person. In the eyes of God, who created us, we are all "good."

But no matter how good we are, we can sometimes make bad choices. We can grow apart from God, and forget what is important in our lives. Going to Mass helps us stay connected to God and to what's important. It nourishes our hearts and souls with God's loving presence and the company of others. It helps us make more loving choices, so that we love as God loves. The Mass helps us get our priorities straight and gives us some time and space where we can be truly ourselves.

Some people say they don't need to go to Mass to be with God. They can be with God at home or in nature. It's true that we can find God anywhere. Personal time for prayer and reflection is blessed time no matter where it happens. But going to Mass is different. It's about being a Christian for the world, not just for ourselves. United as the people of God, we are sent into our communities to continue the healing and teaching work of Jesus. The Mass gives us the strength, guidance and inspiration we need to share our time and our gifts with the world.

If we want to do something for our community, first we need to show up in our community. We start at Mass. The Church is not just the priest and the building. It's a community of God's people working together to continue the work of Jesus in our beautiful but broken world.

# What if I disagree with something the Church says? Should I still go to Mass?

The Church has teachings on many different issues. You could spend a lifetime trying to understand them all. Wise and holy people have spent years, or even centuries, discovering how best to express these official teachings. But the heart of our faith can be summed up in our key beliefs. We find most of these beliefs in the Apostles' Creed. If you can say the Apostles' Creed and believe it, then you share the basic faith of the Church. If you can say the Apostles' Creed, accept other Church teachings, and want to believe but still have questions, then you still belong in the Church!

Questioning is a natural part of learning. Before we turn away from something that the Church teaches, we must ask ourselves some serious questions: Do I really understand Church teachings on this issue? Have I read them, read about them, and talked to someone who understands them? Have I prayed about them?

God calls us to grow in love and wisdom. We bring our questions to Mass with us as we humbly present ourselves to God. Our encounter with the sacred at Mass gives us spiritual strength to face our questions about Church teachings with open minds and open hearts.

## If I have questions or doubts about my faith, who can I talk to?

The Bible is full of stories about people who questioned their faith in God. Time after time, people have cried out, wondering if God is there. So you are not alone if you have questions or doubts. Even Mother Teresa, who spent her life serving others, sometimes had doubts!

There are lots of caring people who can help you with your questions. Start with your parents, your godparents or other members of your family. Even if they can't answer your questions, they can help you put your thoughts into words. (Your friends can listen, too, but they probably can't give you a full answer. They're still learning, like you!) If you go to a Catholic school, try talking to your teacher. At church, you can ask a catechist – someone who teaches religious education. And of course a priest or his assistant can help you find some answers.

Doubts are healthy. You're at a time in your life when you are deciding a lot of things for yourself, including what to believe. Doubts and questions can help make your faith stronger, because they lead you to find out more about your faith.

Don't forget the power of prayer if you are feeling unsure about your faith. Open up your heart to God. Remember that God always answers our prayers, but sometimes in ways we don't expect.

If you haven't been to Mass for a while, think about going to the priest for the sacrament of Reconciliation. You can talk to him about your thoughts and concerns.

Do some research about the Mass online or at the library. Tell a friend or family member something you learn that you didn't know before.

Set aside a few minutes each day to have a conversation with God in prayer. There are lots of ways to pray: say a prayer that you know, like the Our Father; read a story about Jesus in the Bible and picture yourself as one of the characters; sit quietly and say a prayer word over and over in your mind; or ask God to bless you as you begin your day. You can pray anytime and anywhere. God is always listening.

# THE ORDER OF THE MASS

## INTRODUCTORY RITES

Entrance Procession: Hymn
Greeting
Rite of Blessing and Sprinkling Holy Water *or* Penitential Rite
Kyrie
Gloria
Opening Prayer

## LITURGY OF THE WORD

First Reading
Responsorial Psalm
Second Reading
Alleluia or Gospel Acclamation
Gospel
Homily
Profession of Faith: the Creed
General Intercessions / Prayer of the Faithful

## LITURGY OF THE EUCHARIST

Presentation of the Gifts / Preparation of the Altar
Prayer over the Gifts
Eucharistic Prayer: Holy, Holy
                    Memorial Acclamation
                    Great Amen
Communion Rite: Lord's Prayer (Our Father)
                Sign of Peace
                Breaking of the Bread
                Communion
                Prayer after Communion

## CONCLUDING RITE

Blessing
Dismissal

**Alb:** A white linen robe that a priest or deacon wears for Mass over his regular clothes.

**Altar:** The large table at the front of the church. The priest celebrates the Mass from the altar.

**Altar server:** A person (often a young person) who assists the priest during Mass.

**Amen:** What we say at the end of a prayer to show that we agree with the words of the prayer.

**Apostles' Creed:** A statement of Catholic belief in God. It begins with the words "I believe …"

**Baptism:** The sacrament that welcomes people into the Catholic Church.

**Blessing:** A prayer asking for God's love to be shown to people.

**Cassock:** A long gown that priests and bishops wear.

**Chalice:** The cup that holds the wine that the Holy Spirit transforms into Christ's blood during Mass.

**Chasuble:** A long outer robe that the priest wears during Mass.

**Christian Scriptures:** The books in the Bible that tell the story of Jesus and the early Church. This part of the Bible is also known as the New Testament.

**Ciborium:** A container with a lid that holds the consecrated bread.

**Congregation:** The people who are present at Mass.

**Consecration:** The action of changing the bread and wine into the body and blood of Christ.

**Creed:** A statement of belief.

**Deacon:** A man who assists the priest at Mass and presides over some other sacraments. The deacon cannot consecrate the bread and wine.

**Eucharist:** The sacrament where we remember Jesus' last supper with his disciples. At the Eucharist, the priest offers the gifts and calls upon the Holy Spirit to consecrate (make holy) the bread and wine so that Jesus becomes present in these signs. "The Eucharist" can also mean the consecrated bread and wine.

**Eucharistic Prayer:** The prayer the priest prays to consecrate the bread and wine.

**Gloria:** The great hymn to God that we sing after the Penitential Rite.

**Hebrew Scriptures:** The first part of the Bible. It includes the story and wisdom of the Jewish people. It is also called the Old Testament.

**Holy water:** Water that has been blessed. Holy water is used in Baptism and other rituals.

**Host:** The consecrated bread of the Eucharist.

**Hymn:** A song of praise and thanksgiving to God.

**Incense:** Sweet-smelling smoke that is a symbol of holiness.

**Intercession:** A prayer to God that we pray during the Prayer of the Faithful.

**Judaism:** The religion of the Jewish people.

**Kyrie:** The hymn that we sing at the end of the Penitential Rite, asking God to have mercy on us.

**Lamb of God:** One of the names we have for Jesus.

**Lectionary:** The book of readings from the Bible that we listen to during Mass.

**Little sign of the cross:** Making the sign of the cross with your thumb on your forehead, lips and heart. We make this sign before we listen to the Gospel.

**Liturgy:** The public worship of the Church, including the Eucharist.

**Mass:** The celebration of the Eucharist.

**Minister of communion:** A person who helps the priest give out communion.

**New Testament:** The Christian Scriptures, which tell the story of Jesus and the early Church.

**Nicene Creed:** A statement of Christian belief. It begins with the words "We believe …"

**Offertory procession:** The part of the Mass where the bread and wine are brought to the altar.

**Old Testament:** The Hebrew Scriptures, which tell the story of the Jewish people and God.

**Parish:** The local community of the Church.

**Penitential Rite:** A time during the first part of the Mass when we tell God that we are sorry for the things we have done that have distanced us from God, others or ourselves.

**Petition:** One of the prayers of the faithful, where we ask for God's help.

**Prayer:** Talking to God and listening to God. Prayer is a two-way conversation!

**Prayer of the Faithful:** The petitions we make to God.

**Preface:** The opening prayers of the Eucharistic Prayer.

**Responsorial psalm:** The Psalm that follows the first reading. It includes a verse that the congregation says or sings together.

**Rite:** A ritual.

**Ritual:** An action that has deep meaning. Baptism is a ritual. Water is poured on the person as a sign of new life in Christ.

**Sabbath:** The day of rest and worship for the Jewish people. The Sabbath begins on Friday at sunset and ends on Saturday at sunset.

**Sacrament:** Visible sign and action of God's love celebrated in the Catholic Church. There are seven sacraments: Baptism, Confirmation, Reconciliation, Eucharist, Holy Orders, Marriage, and Anointing of the Sick.

**Sacramentary:** The book of prayers that the priest prays during Mass.

**Sacristy:** The small room to the side of the altar where the priest and others prepare for Mass.

**Surplice:** A short alb or white linen robe.

**Tabernacle:** The place where consecrated hosts are kept in between Masses.

**Worship:** The act of giving God honour, thanks and praise.

 **Recycled**
Supporting responsible use
of forest resources
www.fsc.org Cert no. SGS-COC-003153
© 1996 Forest Stewardship Council
FSC